Succeeding with
Difficult
People

THE NO NONSENSE LIBRARY

NO NONSENSE CAREER GUIDES

Managing Time
No Nonsense Management
How to Choose a Career
How to Re-enter the Workforce
How to Write a Resume
No Nonsense Interviewing
Succeeding with Difficult People

NO NONSENSE FINANCIAL GUIDES

How to Use Credit and Credit Cards
Investing in Mutual Funds
Investing in the Stock Market
Investing in Tax Free Bonds
Understanding Money Market Funds
Understanding IRA's
Understanding Treasury Bills and Other U.S. Government Securities
Understanding Common Stocks
Understanding Stock Options and Futures Markets
Understanding Social Security
Understanding Insurance
How to Plan and Invest for Your Retirement
Making a Will and Creating Estate Plans
Understanding Condominiums and Co-ops
How to Buy a Home
Understanding Mortgages and Home Equity Loans

NO NONSENSE SUCCESS GUIDES

NO NONSENSE HEALTH GUIDES

NO NONSENSE COOKING GUIDES

NO NONSENSE PARENTING GUIDES

NO NONSENSE CAR GUIDES

NO NONSENSE CAREER GUIDE™

Succeeding with Difficult People

Katina Z. Jones

To Louis
for his patience and
Dad for his support,
and to my family,
both old and new.

Copyright © 1992 by Longmeadow Press

Published by Longmeadow Press, 201 High Ridge Road, Stamford, CT 06904. All rights reserved. No part of this book may be reproduced or utilized in any form or by any means, electronic or mechanical, including photocopying, recording or by any information storage and retrieval system, without permission in writing from the Publisher.

Cover design by Nancy Sabato

Interior design by Richard Oriolo

ISBN: 0-681-41547-9
Printed in the United States of America
First Edition
0 9 8 7 6 5 4 3 2 1

Acknowledgments

Special thanks to D. E. Liverance, a Michigan psychologist whose name spells out exactly what she is; Margo Nichols for her invaluable assistance with this project and the previous one; Michelle LeComte for her unwavering support; and Frank Weimann for being in New York—so I don't have to.

Contents

Part I

Where the Wild Ones Are

Introduction:
Who Difficult People
Are, and Where You
Might Find Them

Your husband is a Catatonic Unresponsive and you feel you must take his pulse to be sure he's alive and listening to you.

Your co-worker is a Bully, who barricades you in the office and won't let you go until you say, "You know, you're absolutely right."

Your landlord is a Whiner-Complainer, who calls every month the day before the rent is due and says, "Ohhh, do you think you'll be paying the rent on time?"

Your brother and your neighbor are both Know-it-alls,

and they are starting to drive you crazy with their smug closed-mindedness.

Are these new astrological signs? Unfortunately, they're not. They are four of the eight most common types of difficult people. When you run into one you often say, "I just want to *strangle* him," even though you know you don't mean it.

This book is expressly intended for people, like you, who would like to learn how to keep their blood pressure down when they deal with difficult people. It offers examples of different situations that may arise when difficult people are around and suggests strategies for dealing with each one.

This book also tells you how to develop and use assertiveness and a sense of humor as both preventive and protective methods, and it offers advice on how to avoid becoming a difficult person yourself—a knee-jerk reaction that's all too common when dealing with people who are being difficult.

Let's begin with brief definitions of each of these types.

The Whiner-Complainer

Perhaps the type most offensive to others, Whiner-Complainers put people off merely by the sound of their voice. Their sentences usually begin with either a heavy sigh or a drawn out "Ohhh . . ." spoken in a peevish tone. Once you've heard it, you'll never forget what it sounds like.

Whiners can usually be found in crowded places, such as shopping malls, grocery stores, and movie theaters and, quite often, appear in government offices—since these can offer the greatest reasons for complaining.

The Know-it-all

Know-it-alls, obviously, are convinced they know every-thing about . . . well, everything. They are never open to the suggestions, ideas, or experiences of others. They have a cool, smug air, gesture often, and usually begin sentences with "If I'm right about this," or "Let me point out . . ."

This type runs a close second to the Whiner on the offensiveness scale and turns up just about anywhere. (After all, they know *everything*.)

The Overzealous Competitor

The Overzealous Competitor most often found in office situations, and is also known as the "Office Brownnose." Almost every office has one. These people are ruthlessly competitive to the point that they will call attention to the small mistakes of others in order to make themselves look better to the boss.

Memos are a favorite way of achieving such treachery; keeping notes on other employees is another.

More often than not, the Overzealous Competitor has grown into this type after a lifetime as an overachiever. In their youth, they got to read the school news over the P.A. system and were always referred to by the principal as "such good kids" because they acted as informants against other students. I'm sure you remember the type.

The Catatonic Unresponsive

Catatonic Unresponsives are hard to diagnose at first, mainly because you're not sure whether they are actually alive. This type seems to be listening to what you're saying, but fails to show any sign or acknowledgment of it—not even a grunt or a sigh. The subject merely sits there, barely breathing, forcing the speaker to constantly say things like, ". . . you know?" or "Are you with me?"

This one is most often found in your own home, and is usually leaning back in a recliner.

The Bully

Every time you're around a Bully you feel as though you're going to get beaten up if you don't agree with everything this person is saying.

Characterized by their mean looks and other, more grandiose nonverbal cues (all of which indicate their need for total dominance), these are people who will not let you out of the room until you say, "You know, umm, you're absolutely right."

The Bully can appear anywhere, and usually manifests itself after several beers.

The Non-Listener

A fine difference exists between the Catatonic Unresponsive and the Non-Listener. The Catatonic type is, much to your surprise, actually listening to what you're saying. Non-Listeners, on the other hand, do not hear a word you're saying because they're too busy trying to figure out what to say next themselves.

They never give eye contact, and they interrupt often, many times not even realizing they're doing it. The most annoying tendency they have, however, is talking over another person who's already engaged in a conversation.

Non-Listeners have one strikingly apparent characteristic: They ask the same question repeatedly because they never listened to your answer the first time. (There are shared elements with the Know-it-all type.)

The Non-Listener is commonly found in homes and offices—definitely a socially handicapped individual.

The Hopelessly Impatient

Hopelessly Impatient ones always show up early for social engagements, then complain that you're "running late." They sigh heavily, switch the weight of their bodies from foot to foot relentlessly and, in worst-case scenarios, begin taking on characteristics of the other types.

The Hopelessly Impatient can be found in shopping malls, grocery stores, amusement parks, and anywhere else you might be forced to stand in line.

This type is the most clear-cut example of how much an "instant gratification" society we've become.

The Volcano

True to its name, the Volcano will erupt at the drop of a hat; it often explodes first and apologizes later.

Most often, this type is found in the office, but it can also appear at home. Volcanos are not often seen in public places because they prefer one-on-one confrontations as opposed to mass demonstrations of their temper.

The sad thing is, many times these people are not even aware of their flare-ups until after the fact, which makes it even more difficult for those around them.

Okay. But How Can I Change These People?

You can't change these people. But you can change the way you deal with them, instead of just wanting to strangle them. This book will teach you that, by using several simple strategies coupled with a healthy dose of humor, you can change the effect these people are having on you.

What This Book Won't Do for You

This book won't make difficult people disappear from your life. Its cardinal rule is: You cannot avoid difficult people, you can only avoid difficult situations with these people.

As you endeavor to overcome the stress that so often arises from having to work with or live with difficult people, you will learn that you can only be responsible for how you react to a person or situation.

No one *makes* you feel like attempting strangulation; this is the way you *choose* to respond to the Bully in your office or the Know-it-all neighbor—only you are responsible for your reaction.

You can decide to behave differently.

You can choose to ignore the Whiner in the apartment next to yours.

You can learn how to interact with the Overzealous Competitor in a healthy, nonthreatening manner.

You can learn how to express your feelings calmly and in a way that allows you and the difficult person to really communicate.

The key is first to know what you'd like to accomplish with each of these eight difficult types. Then you can go about the business of achieving it responsibly.

**Everyone has an inherent right
to be treated with courtesy and dignity.**

Assertive people know who they are, know their human boundaries, and act accordingly in a quiet, self-confident way. But aggressive people tend to exceed their human boundaries, pretend to be more than what they are, grab the things they want, and pick fights with other people merely for the sport of it. Assertive people make their point only after listening to all sides of a matter, while aggressive people try to dominate the entire conversation. Assertive people are good listeners; aggressive ones only wish to hear themselves speak.

In short, assertive people have true self-confidence, while aggressive people mistakenly think they do.

Self-confidence is important because it is your major line of defense. Self-confident people aren't attacked by the difficult ones—mostly because the Bullys or the Whiners can sense that they will promptly be put back in their place. Mind you, I am not saying that self-confident people should resort to Bully-like behavior in order to demonstrate their powers—on the contrary. The truly self-confident don't need to put on airs of superiority; it is not their goal to be superior—just to be the best they can possibly be.

But self-confidence is not easy to instill because throughout our young lives we were taught to be humble (well, at least *most* of us were) and now we feel guilty for having even a shred of confidence in ourselves and our abilities. We were never really taught the one lesson that could help us most in life. So, we have to learn it by ourselves.

Of course, learning anything by yourself helps build self-confidence, which brings us to the perplexing question of how to gain that confidence in the first place.

Self-confidence comes after you've taken a long, hard look at all the things you do well and all the things you'd just as soon forget about yourself. This involves taking inventory of all the tiny components that make up *you*—and then accepting the things you can't change. Essentially, it entails looking yourself in the eye and saying," I'm okay. I have some faults, like anybody else, but I'm truly working on being the best me I can. And that's all I can ever do."

The thing most difficult people, especially the Bully and the Volcano, look for in their victims is a lack of confidence. This gives them carte blanche because they know they can get away with attacking you since you're not equipped to defend yourself properly or to set limits on which types of behavior you will, and will not, put up with.

You must recognize that it is your responsibility to see to it that you are not taken advantage of, ever. You alone set the boundaries.

Remember: You cannot change difficult people, only the way they affect you. You can try to enlighten them a bit about their annoying or disruptive behavior, but they alone have the responsibility of changing for the better.

Being assertive is your best way of dealing with difficult people, and knowing what assertive people are like is your primary key to becoming one yourself.

Common Traits of Assertive People

Assertive people have several traits in common. Among these are

- The ability to present their ideas without fear or shyness.
- A genuine concern for the thoughts and opinions of others, which encourages a fair exchange of ideas.

- Certain physical signs like direct eye contact, posture that is straight yet leans in toward the other person, and positive facial expressions, which are displayed only when genuine—not merely to be polite.
- The rare ability to present an idea and then pause effectively—so that other person may speak.
- The ability to see a situation objectively. This means that all pettiness about previous events or personality conflicts (e.g., "I can see now why your first wife divorced you") are *not* brought into the discussion.

Assertive people possess a quiet confidence, an almost indescribable peace within. They seem to have both feet firmly planted on the ground despite trials and obstacles and seem to know that everything will be all right, even if it's not evident at the present time.

They are in touch with their needs, wants, and opinions, and believe that everyone, including themselves, deserves respect and courtesy.

Assertive people also know when to stop a discussion that seems to be going nowhere—usually with a positive suggestion like, "Let's talk about this tomorrow, when we can cool down and discuss the problem in a mature way."

A Final Checklist

Now that you know what assertive behavior is, and you've decided to begin the work of becoming assertive, here are seven questions to ask yourself when attempting to deal with difficult people. Try to go over these on a daily basis for a while in order to familiarize yourself with the thinking processes of an assertive person. Train your brain with these thoughts. And, if you'd like, try keeping them in a journal. Write out these questions and their answers for each difficult situation you encounter.

1. Have I listened thoroughly to this person's gripes?
2. Have I reacted in a calm manner?
3. Have I taken into account what this person's underlying fears or concerns might be?
4. Have I avoided placing blame and instead talked about how to correct the situation—for the good of all?
5. Have I presented my own ideas or concerns in a helpful, positive manner?
6. Have I maintained my sense of humor and tried to be an inspiration to others around me, including the difficult person?
7. Has every possible option been fully explored and attempted?

Good luck, and may the force of assertiveness be with you as you continue to encounter difficult people throughout your life.

One

Assertiveness Can Help

Many think that the most important tool to have on hand when dealing with difficult people is a chain saw, or maybe a machete. But self-confidence and assertiveness are really the two tools you need. If you have these, difficult people can't get to you as easily.

Assertiveness is often confused with aggressiveness, and wrongly so. Aggressiveness connotes a kind of reaching (possibly in an arrogant manner) for what you believe ought to be yours, while assertiveness simply means that you stand up for yourself when necessary, and show a little confidence.

**Difficult people often aren't aware
that they're hurting the people close
to them. Your objective is to
find common ground, then work
toward a mutual understanding.**

Two

!%*#/!
Be the Tie That
Binds

Whether or not we like to admit it, sometimes family members can be the most annoying and difficult people that we will ever come across.

That's because of all the people we interact with, we're probably with them the most.

And though an individual family's problems may seem unique, these are, in fact, as universal as human beings themselves.

Television and print advertising have misled us into believing that the perfect family never fights and, if it does, the fight only lasts thirty to sixty minutes. Overcoming

Part II

Dealing with Difficult Family and Friends

these unrealistic expectations is the first step in dealing with difficult relatives.

Sibling Rivalry

My sister always tries to one-up me in everything. We just had a birthday party for our five-year-old at a local restaurant, so she planned her child's next party at a nicer one. She constantly tries to out-do my brother, too, and spends a lot of money doing things that weren't necessary to begin with. We both love her, but she's really getting on our nerves! We can't understand why she feels the need to act like this.

—*Janet G.*

Some of us never outgrow that early childhood syndrome, "Mom-loved-you-best." And the Overzealous Competitor is at the top of that list.

The important thing to keep in mind is that you can't lower yourself to the level of constantly competing against your own relatives (or anyone else, for that matter). So, instead of entering into combat with like behavior, try finding out why the Competitor is feeling the need to compete.

At a time when you are together, away from your other relatives, ask why the Competitor feels inferior. Remind them that everyone feels inferior at one time or another and most of the time such worries are completely unfounded.

Then, think of all the positive and reassuring comments you can tell the Competitor. They desperately need to be reminded of their good points, and this will help move the conversation on to the next step, which is a specific discussion about what kinds of negative behavior need to be changed into positive behavior.

For every example of negative behavior you bring up, be prepared to offer a positive suggestion. For instance, in the case of the child's birthday party, offer a suggestion like, "Why not have it at the same restaurant? The kids had a really good time there and it would help keep things on an even keel between us and between the kids. After all, we don't want to teach them to compete, do we?"

Above all else, don't be fooled into thinking that you don't need to tell Overzealous Competitors their good points. Too often, people shrug this off with a "they-already-know-that." The fact is, even if they do know it, Overzealous Competitors need reassurance on a fairly regular basis.

Besides, who ever gets tired of hearing positive things about themselves?

I Married a What?

My husband just turns on the T.V. and sits back in his recliner when he gets home from work. He doesn't really respond to much of what I say to him. Occasionally, I'll hear a grunt, but for the most part, he just lies there throwing me blank stares. I desperately need to have daily interaction with this man I married—but more than half the time I wind up having to take his pulse to see if he's still alive. I don't know how to get him back into the land of the living.

—Suzanne E.

Catatonic Unresponsives are not the lively sorts that so many of their relatives wish they were but, more often than not, there is an outside cause for their behavior (or lack thereof).

Is your "zoned-out" relative stressed out over work? Ask what a typical day is like. The answer might be your first clue to the innate unhappiness that often leads to Catatonic Unresponsive behavior. A stressful work situation can take the wind out of even normal people's sails and render them totally useless by the end of each day.

But, you protest, is that any excuse for my being virtually ignored? No, it isn't. But there are ways to deal with the Catatonic Unresponsive—a difficult person who, more than any other type, probably needs your help.

First, you need to ask a lot of questions. Mind you, these cannot be questions that can be answered with a simple yes or no. These *must* be open-ended questions, like: "What specifically tires you out during the day or stresses you to the point of total withdrawal?" or "How can I help you learn to relax at the end of the day?"

Then, ask the Catatonic Unresponsive to make a list of all known stressors, and next to each one, to write their causes and positive solutions. Sometimes it's hard for people to come up with positive solutions off the top of their heads. Having them ask the question, "What do I wish could happen next time?" can be a good launching pad.

All the while, reassure the Catatonic Unresponsive that you're only trying to help. Never criticize the behavior itself because that will only makes the difficult person withdraw even further. And always be sure to let the Catatonic Unresponsive know what *your* ideal evening would be like, too.

My Brother, the Bully

My brother is a big bully. He makes me feel like he's going to haul off and hit me if I don't agree with whatever he says. He'll say something, then glare at me and ask, 'Right?' I mean, how am I supposed to respond to that? I know if I disagree, he'll argue with me until I give in.

—Philip D.

Bullys are not easy to deal with at all because, although they rather enjoy manipulating others, they don't like feeling manipulated themselves.

Extreme subtlety is important when you approach the Bully with your problem. You cannot let on that you're attempting to fix a problem until you have gotten the Bully to let his or her guard down—and this is not an easy feat.

One way to accomplish this is to wait for the difficult situation to pass, then quietly (and in a nonaccusatory way) express your feelings about your need to know that your ideas will be listened to and sometimes accepted. Ask why the Bully hasn't given you much of a chance to explain yourself in the past.

Don't waste a lot of time blaming the Bully, however. It is *your* problem to deal with because it was *you* who chose to feel hurt. That's okay, though. You needed to do this in order to clear your thoughts and begin to focus on the solution stage.

Finding solutions with Bullys is not easy because for them it means learning how to share the spotlight (so to speak). But if you can persuade the Bully that sharing will bring greater personal rewards, you will find that this beast can be blissfully domesticated.

The Know-it-all at Home

My husband thinks he knows everything. He's so smug. When he says things like, 'If I'm right about this. . . ' or 'Let me point out to you that. . . ' it makes me so mad, I could just scream! I sometimes shoot back that he's not the only one who's right—but then I start feeling guilty for lowering myself to his level. I just wish he would stop being so damned smug!

—Darleen W.

Smugness is the main attribute of the Know-it-all. But being a Know-it-all is a tough job—because you have to keep playing the game that you know everything, even when you don't.

Such compulsive behavior is all too common with the Know-it-all who, like the Overzealous Competitor, needs constant reassurance. People of this type must be convinced that you do think their ideas are important, in spite of your need to present your own thoughts. Remember this before you initiate a discussion to clear the air.

Your first step is to call a meeting. Tell (don't ask) the Know-it-all that you need input on a problem you're trying to solve. (Here you're appealing to the Know-it-all's sense of self-importance.)

Next, make two columns on a piece of paper and write the word "Current" in one and "Future" in the other. (See the following example.) Then, gently tell the Know-it-all that the problem is that you feel your relationship is a bit one-sided and that you're looking for a way to make it more well-balanced. At this point, ask for input.

Current	Future
My perception is that you never listen to my ideas	We need five minutes each to present our ideas, followed by ten minutes of discussion
My perception is that we can never get past petty know-it-all behavior—we both get too angry	We need to remember that we are mature adults and must treat each other with courtesy and respect

Fill in the first column with your perceptions about the current troublesome behavior. Then *both* of you should write your thoughts in the "Future" column. Look for any similarities or differences that still need to be discussed and stress the importance of finding a good compromise. Be assertive about your right to express your thoughts as much as the Know-it-all's.

This kind of thinking on paper will accomplish two things: First, it will direct attention away from each of you, help focus on the problem now before *both* of you, and create an atmosphere of teamwork, a concept previously missing from the mind of the Know-it-all. Second, it will help the Know-it-all see that working together on a problem can be more "right" than either person involved. If you use this exercise every time the Know-it-all strikes, the point will eventually sink in.

The most important thing to do at the end of such an exercise is to say, "You see, we found the right solution together. And now we're *both* right."

The Hopelessly Impatient Relative

Whenever we're going out together my sister-in-law always shows up about twenty minutes early, then harasses me about not being ready. She'll stand at the bottom of the stairs, tapping her foot and saying "C'mon—hurry up!" Usually, we just go to a bar to hear a band we like. They don't even start until 10:30 at night—but she shows up before 9:30! I don't want to hurt her feelings, but this is really getting on my nerves!

—Laurie A.

We all set goals for the kinds of behavior we expect from ourselves and others. Unfortunately, Hopelessly Impatients set unusually high (and often impossible) goals, and then beat themselves up over why they weren't able to meet them.

A Hopelessly Impatient family member needs to be told exactly that: to stop setting goals that cannot be met, and to learn to allow more room to be human. Human beings, after all, are sometimes late.

As in most other difficult heart-to-heart talks, you should sit alone together in a quiet place. In a nonthreatening way, ask the Impatient one why keeping on a tight schedule is so important. Try to avoid accepting a glib answer—never let an "Oh, I don't know" slip by without a little more probing.

You will then want to ask if it's possible for the Hopelessly Impatient one to grant you more space. After all, if you're not on a tight time schedule (dictated by social demands or obligations), why not take a little extra time to make sure that a good time can be had—by *all*?

The Exploding Father

My dad gets so mad at things normal people would just shrug off. The other day, he had stepped out of the family room for a while, so my sister changed the television channel to something she wanted to watch. When he returned, he pitched a major fit. He screamed at her, demanded the television controls back, then apologized to her an hour later after he had cooled down. My sister was pretty upset by his behavior.

—John M.

Volcanos erupt first, then explain or apologize later. It's their one utterly distinguishable trait—and oddly enough, it rarely achieves anything.

If you hope to see more positive behavior from a Volcano, it is better to approach this smokestack in one of its nonactive phases.

Gently state your intentions ("It would be so nice if we could talk out our difficulties instead of blowing up," you might begin.) Watch for a warning—if no red lights go off, you're on the right track.

If you absolutely cannot wait for the Volcano to finish erupting before trying to talk things out, you must tread carefully. Begin by speaking in a very slow, soothing tone. Tell the Volcano that you don't see the need to blow up every time you have a difference of opinion and that, instead, you would prefer to discuss things quietly. If this is not possible, or if the Volcano becomes more hostile as a result of your ability to remain calm (which often happens), then you will simply have to give the Volcano a few minutes alone to calm down.

Active Volcanos usually exhibit all or some of these

strong physical signs of anger: reddened ears and neck, tightened neck and shoulder muscles, and strained facial expressions. As the Volcano dies down these signs will to disappear. When they have, you can make your move.

While it may not seem fair to have to wait for the Volcano to calm down, unfortunately, it is sometimes the only way to get your point safely across. In a worst-case scenario, a Volcano is the one type who might actually physically hurt you—something that, although unpleasant, you must always keep in mind.

Volcanos really need to have their nerves retrained, and this can be accomplished most efficiently by their doing regular exercises immediately after the explosion occurs.

For instance, I know one couple who are both Volcanos. In the past their heated arguments had resulted in broken furniture. Now they "sentence" each other to five complete minutes of telling each other everything they like about the other person.

The first time (which, by the way, is always the most difficult), they burst into laughter three or four minutes into their "sentences." Now they rarely have heated arguments at all—and they've found that they also never have to ask each other that God-awful question, "Why did you marry me, anyway?" This exercise is highly recommended for all family members experiencing difficulties with each other.

The Whining Mate

My husband whines a lot. If he expresses some mild displeasure with the clothes I wear or the food I cook, I'll ask him if everything's okay, but he says everything's fine. I'm willing to change things he doesn't like—if he'd only tell me what they are. Sometimes I think he just likes to hear himself complain. Maybe he thinks it makes him more in control, or something.

—Kate B.

Whiners often behave the way they do in an effort to get attention or gain control over someone. The key is to find out why.

Perhaps your situation is one where your spouse wants both attention and control. Have you been communicating much lately? Has the conversation been meaningful, or just run-of-the-mill? Is there something that you might inadvertently have said or done that could have prompted this negative behavior?

Ask yourself these questions before engaging in a discussion about the behavior. Then, sit in a quiet part of your house (away from distractions) and ask your spouse to list three things that he or she likes about you and dislikes about you. Afterward, you do the same.

This is the point at which you can get to the meat of what's wrong because, more than likely, the problems have just been stated in your list. Then in a calm, detached manner, try to discuss how you might achieve better understanding and mutual happiness. It could very well be that the problem is minor and that a solution can be reached via a compromise (e.g., "I'll stop whining about your dinners because I'll try to remember that I love you for trying to make me happy"). Putting reminders of your agreement on note cards and placing them strategically around the house may sound silly, but often it's very effective.

Take My In-Law—Please

My wife's father never listens to anything we say. He comes over to visit, asks us questions that we never get to answer, then repeats the questions several times—never giving us a chance to speak. Often these questions will contain a brief pause, then a throaty "Huh?" It drives me nuts! My wife says it bothers her as well, but she's learned to put up with it. I, however, dread his visits.

—Howard L.

Non-Listeners can be especially annoying because they never permit you to really interact with them. Maybe they don't like others getting too close—conversation can be such a revealing and intimate way of interacting that they find it far too threatening to even participate.

But this analysis may not go far enough because dealing with a Non-Listener who's a family member can present some additional problems. Not only do you have to rule out the possibility of a serious disease (like Alzheimer's, where short-term memory is affected and those afflicted repeat themselves or don't seem to hear responses to questions), you may also have to contend with the opposing viewpoints of family members, who will try to defend the Non-Listener. No other type invokes such pity and support.

The best thing to do with Non-Listeners is to remove them from their defenders (but only for a little while). Suggest to your Non-Listener that the two of you go for a walk or to a quiet restaurant. Then, ask if you may have the floor for a few minutes to get your point across without interruption. (Be firm about the noninterruption part because the Non-Listener will undoubtedly test you. When the test occurs, clearly say, "I'm not through yet," then continue speaking.)

Tell the Non-Listener that it hurts your feelings that the two of you rarely get a chance to interact. State that by bringing this up all you are hoping to accomplish is a better relationship between you. Then succinctly, yet thoroughly, outline how you would like your future communications to go.

Again, exercises may be helpful. For instance, have the Non-Listener practice giving 30-second pauses after each question. Run practice "drills" from time to time. Making it seem like a game will make it less painful for everyone, and it might even bring you closer.

A Note About Children

Since there are any number of well-written books on dealing with difficult children, this is a topic best left to the experts. Consult your local library or bookstore for a list of current titles.

You cannot change difficult people.
You can only open their eyes to how their
behavior affects others, and gently let them know
you understand that sometimes
it's hard to be human.

Three

Office Antics

If the home is the number-one place where problems with difficult people may arise, then the office runs a close second. Again, this is because you spend a large amount of time with your co-workers, many of whom are fiercely competitive.

Nearly every one of the eight types of difficult people can rear its ugly heads in the office, but five are most common. They present problems we've all had to deal with and must inevitably face again in the future.

Why Office Confrontations Are Bad

Aside from making everyone unhappy, office confrontations are unproductive and a waste of precious company time. As we all know, time is money in the business world, and many a harried executive has spent entire working days trying to solve an office conflict.

If a typical employee is paid $10 an hour, and a typical day is eight hours long, calculate how much a three-hour conflict between four employees can cost the company. That $120 may not seem like much in the grand scheme of the business world, but if you multiply it by twenty occurrences per year, you're looking at some pretty pricey arguments—$2,400.

If you imagine how your boss would look at you if you wrongfully took $2,400 from the company, then you'll begin to see why it is that most bosses frown upon the unproductive variety of in-house arguing.

When Can Office
Confrontations Be Productive?

Office confrontations, on a small and controlled scale, can be productive when they clear the air between employees who were not communicating effectively prior to the confrontation.

Mind you, when I use the word "confrontation" here, I'm not referring to loud, boisterous screaming matches. Instead, I mean a brief acknowledgment of your differences in opinion, followed by a discussion of exactly where those differences occur and how best to achieve harmony or a compromise. This kind of teamwork is paramount to solving social conflicts in the workplace and making it a better place for everyone.

The Office Volcano

A man in my office blows up at the drop of a hat, then storms his way back to his office, slamming the door behind him. It usually happens after our strategic planning meetings on Mondays. Other co-workers have begun to recognize this pattern. How can we make him stop doing this? It creates quite a stir, and renders most of us unproductive for at least half an hour afterward. Inevitably, someone (usually me) goes to his office and calmly asks what's wrong, only to be told to go away.

—Laura C.

The most dangerous and disruptive force in the office is the Volcano. This is the easiest type of difficult person to spot, and yet the most complicated to understand.

Who can say exactly what motivates Volcanos? (Usually, their co-workers are afraid to get close enough to find out.) It could be personal problems, fear of inadequacy, or mental flashbacks of bad situations. Worse yet, it could be a sign of mental burnout or a chemical dependency problem.

In the case of the office Volcano whose eruptiveness is not caused by chemical problems, the best solution is, right off the bat, to say that their behavior is unacceptable. Then, wait for the Volcano to cool down before attempting a serious discussion about the problem. (Note: Cool-down periods can be as brief as three minutes or last as long as a few days, depending on the person. Unfortunately, you must play things by ear.)

Addressing the immediate problem can be easy. All you have to say to the Volcano is, "You're way out of line," or "Why don't we discuss this again when you can respond in a more mature manner?" Such minor scolding on your part is not a negative thing to do because it instantly alerts the Volcano to the fact that he or she might be behaving badly.

Giving Volcanos time and space to cool down is the second essential element. Suggest that they take a walk outside or get a drink of water. If necessary, offer to bring water to their office so they can have some quiet time alone.

After the cool-down period is over (you can tell by an open office door or by the Volcano's popping in to apologize—which, by the way, they often do), then you can proceed to the next step: a calm discussion of the fact that such outbursts upset the other workers and waste valuable time. Ask why the Volcano feels such behavior will accomplish anything and, more important, why it is that he or she cannot control such temper flare-ups.

You can end the discussion by offering to help in whatever way you can. Or, offer your assistance in finding a qualified professional who can help the Volcano through what may be a personally difficult time.

In fact, you might be surprised to learn that as many as eight out of ten Volcanos suffer from a deep hurt that has little to do with the office. Understanding is what the Volcano needs most, followed by continued encouragement.

Obviously, chemically dependent or mentally fatigued Volcanos also need to be told of their problems and helped as much as company policy allows. These cases always require documentation of the events that occurred, including descriptions of the perpetrator's behavior, and brief statements as to what particular actions were taken to address the individual's problems.

The Bully at Work

Whenever my boss and I have one-on-one meetings to discuss certain operating procedures and other company concerns, she pressures me into agreeing with almost everything she says. For instance, when the topic of flex time came up, she presented her points and then repeatedly told me she was correct on every one of them. She never asks for my opinion, and when I volunteer it an argument always ensues, and she inevitably wears me down into saying she's absolutely right. Now I've found that I agree with everything she says just to get her off my back. I don't see any other way around this.

—Donald G.

There's nothing Bullys like more than when their "subjects" give in without an argument because that tells them that they can win without even having to fight—which reinforces their belief in their own superiority.

Bullys operate on two levels—verbal and nonverbal. Their verbal side manifests itself with their constant "you-know"s, "know-what-I'm-saying"s, and "understand-that"s. All of these phrases are designed to induce agreement from the subject. Their nonverbal characteristics include grandiose gesturing like waving their arms about in the air indicating their need for dominance) and the closing of doors (indicating that there's no escape until you surrender).

You must realize that on a basic human level there is a very fine line between feelings of superiority and feelings of inferiority. Bullys often seem to be motivated by an overwhelming superiority complex, when, in fact, the very reason they need to assert themselves in this manner is to prove to themselves that they are not inferior. What an odd game, you might say. But understanding that this is their basic motivating force, strangely opposite to what it at first seemed to be, will help you in your quest to end the "battle of the Bully."

Armed with the knowledge that what Bullys worry most about is being inferior, you can now approach them feeling that you are on common ground. We've all experienced inferiority complexes of some sort, so keep this in mind when you walk into the Bully's office to talk about "the difficulty" you're having. (Remember, it is your problem, too—only you're looking for a happy solution.)

Entering the "Torture Chamber"

First, ask the Bully to please set aside a few minutes to talk about a pressing matter. You'll probably get an immediate response because such a request appeals to the Bully's sense of superiority.

Next, insist that you sit in chairs next to each other, thereby removing the desk that acts as a class barrier. Now you are ready to talk on the same, human level.

Offer your picture of the situation. Be ready with vivid examples to combat the question, "When was I like this?" Always, always stress that teamwork is a key element to a productive office. Put it in the greater context of the business world and you should be able to find common ground, and a solution will then be possible.

The Overzealous Competitor
Strikes Again

My immediate superior keeps a notebook where he records certain things either I or other co-workers have said or done—all completely out of context. It seems everything we say or do eventually comes back in our faces. Not only does he keep this notebook, he also keeps a time log of our comings and goings during the day (including lunches and trips to the rest room). Twice in our company-wide meetings he's brought up the fact that some co-workers leave "up to nine minutes early." Will this petty behavior ever stop?
—Kathy J.

The Overzealous Competitor (also known as the "Office Brownnose") is in constant need of one "fix" more than any other: approval from the boss or an immediate supervisor. As with the Bully, more than likely this stems from an inferiority complex; and yet, it goes even deeper than that.

Many Overzealous Competitors suffer from an innate need or desire to be better than everyone else—at least in *some*thing. Their behavior is usually an overcompensation for some other perceived deficiency or shortcoming. If you can find out what the Overzealous Competitor believes is "wrong" with him or her self then, with supportive comments or understanding words, you can begin to help heal that particular wound; . Soon, the Overzealous Competitor will achieve a better personality balance—and usually the difficult behavior will stop as well.

Winning the Battle, But Not the War

The best you can hope for in these situations is winning the battle, not the war. And, unfortunately, co-workers lower on the totem pole than the Overzealous Competitor cannot do much to protect themselves without lowering themselves to this kind of backstabbing.

I once handled a similar situation by waiting until the Competitor was out on a vacation day, and then I took his notebook. I photocopied as much of the purloined notebook as possible, and and then I presented it to his boss along with a formal rebuttal of the allegations against me. One copy ended up in my personnel file with a complimentary note from the higher-up, and the other wound up in his file with a not-so-sparkling note about counterproductive and paranoid behavior.

In the end, this Overzealous Competitor only succeeded in making himself look bad.

The Know-it-all

My business partner is convinced that he's right about every aspect of running our company. He's always saying things like "I just know I'm right about this" and then complimenting himself out loud when he is right about something. Whenever I try to bring up new business strategies for discussion, he always acts like he's the boss, and sometimes he openly rejects my ideas before I even get a chance to express them. It's really annoying, especially for me. Now even the receptionist is beginning to notice his behavior. She asked me the other day who the real boss is.

—Jim B.

Know-it-alls are the most difficult of the eight difficult types to approach with any idea, let alone a good one, because ideas presented by other people alert Know-it-alls to the fact that they may not always be right. That is the toughest pill for Know-it-alls to swallow.

Know-it-alls have another trait that all too often gives them away: They repeatedly bring up their credentials; "Listen, I got my M.B.A. from Harvard—I know a bad business deal when I see one"; "A Ph.D. in physics hasn't failed me yet."

Is this yet another example of an inferiority complex at work? Well, yes . . . and no. Yes, because the Know-it-all's major (and usually most unrealistic) fear in life is being exposed as a person who knows nothing at all. And no, because sometimes the Know-it-all is merely a person who has the best intentions at heart.

For instance, the difficult business associate in the example above may have a lot of experience and may also be looking to save time; perhaps his business associate tends to talk on and on about ideas, taking up more time at every meeting than is necessary.

But what if this person simply is an annoying Know-it-all? How would you deal with that? Would you get impatient, but bottle your emotions until you became a Volcano? Or would you just smile and nod, your stomach churning inside?

Neither way is correct. The most effective way to deal with the office Know-it-all is to sit quietly together and dissect the problem, like this:

- YOU: You know, Bob, I have some ideas I'd really like to discuss with you. They'll only take about five minutes of your time.
- BOB (a.k.a. Know-it-all): Why? Haven't we already discussed what we're going to do?
- YOU: (calmly) Not exactly. What we did discuss were

your ideas on the topic. But I think it's only fair I should get the opportunity to present mine. After all, we are a team here, right?

• BOB: (reluctantly) Yessss. (pause) Well, okay, go ahead.

At this point look for physical cues that he's still listening. For instance, his posture should be straight, not slouching and, if you're facing each other, he should be leaning in just a little bit toward you. His pupils will be wide, and he should remain quietly responsive until you are through.

You needn't remind him of any deep-seated reasons behind his Know-it-all–hood—that would only put him further on the defensive. His guard must be down for you to deal effectively with him or with any of the other eight types of difficult people.

Ohh, Noooo . . . Not the Whiner

One of the other secretaries in my office complains about everything and whines about being underpaid and over-worked. Yet, she and I work the same amount of hours each day for the exact same salary. I am satisfied with my job and feel that the pay here is better than in two of my previous jobs.

The other day, Jill said rather loudly, "Why–y–y do I have to do that? Oh, what a complete waste of time!" after her boss asked her to retype an order that had changed. We are all getting pretty fed up with these outbursts, and yet we still feel sorry enough for her that we want to talk to her about her behavior. But how can we do this?

—Cheryl R.

Whiners are the most patience-intensive, time-consuming types of difficult people to work with. They tend to complain about everything, and they always do it in a loud, obvious manner.

Not only are they negative people to be around in general, but they are also slightly futilistic. This means that they "can't see the point" to completing those at-times-boring tasks that must be done to keep the office running.

Barring chronic/clinical depression (a serious condition that requires the care of a licensed professional) as the cause of the whining and complaining, the main affliction of this particular type is that they prefer wallowing in their self-made muck rather than rising above their situations. This is why few, if any, Whiners are ever promoted to positions of importance or power.

Many Whiners feel they don't deserve much in life, and when (because of their own actions) they don't receive much, they instinctively believe it's because they aren't good enough—they knew it all along. It's like a sign lights up within them, saying, "See, you were right. You're not worth that raise, so you shouldn't try anymore."

Understanding this negative self-image will help you learn to deal with the Whiner-Complainer. Your first move is to invite the Whiner to a casual lunch. At this lunch, start by saying something like, "You know, I've noticed that you're unhappy here. What do you see as the problem, and how can I help you solve it?" This is the kind of open-ended question that begs an answer—and the answer will lead to a better understanding between you and your co-worker.

Your final step is to ask what the Whiner sees as wrong with him or her self. Whiners always know the answer to that question, even though they might be reluctant to share it. Patience and compassion are your two strongest allies here.

Remember, as with every other type, the Whiner-Complainer is really just reaching out, trying to be understood.

A Last Resort

Although it is the last resort, if a co-worker persists in being difficult, often the only way for a manager to solve that particular conflict permanently is by terminating the employee.

In such a case, you may be called upon to produce dated records of the problems that have occurred along with complete descriptions of how the employee was being difficult.

It may not be a bad idea of you to keep such a record for yourself, too. (The following chart is a good example.) In one column, write the perpetrator's name; in the second, write the date the event occurred. In the third column, describe the actions and words that back up your labeling this person as "difficult." But in the fourth and final column, enter descriptions of your own behavior.

It may astonish you to find that you haven't been a complete angel, either.

Name	Date	Actions	My Behavior
Chad R.	7/10	Slammed door	Tried to calm him down
Chad R.	9/19	Yelled at boss	Warned him; offered help
Chad R.	10/20	Threw ashtray	Got angry at him; then felt guilty

**They key words to remember when you
encounter difficult people are
"calmness" and "patience."**

Four

"But This Is My Vacation!" Avoiding "Excess Baggage"

How many times have you gone on a vacation to relax and get away from stress, only to find more stress on the road to your supposed "haven"?

Difficult people can turn your "dream vacation" into a living nightmare. Whether it's the hotel desk clerk who refuses to do anything about your botched reservation, your wife complaining about the long car ride, or the man sitting next to you on the tour bus who constantly complains about the scenery, this chapter will offer tips on how to keep these intruders from ruining your time "away from it all."

The Hopelessly Impatient Traveler

My wife and I are going on another vacation soon. We can't afford to fly, so we're driving six-hundred miles. The problem is, every time we get on the road, she starts asking me right away how long it will take to get there. When we make rest stops, she tells me to hurry. Also, she's constantly looking at the speedometer to make sure I'm driving fast enough. Last year, when we went to check into our hotel, the desk clerk had lost our reservation and my wife went berserk. I'm hoping that won't happen again, because it really embarrassed me.

—Mark S.

The Hopelessly Impatient traveler never quite grew out of the "are-we-there-yet?" phase of childhood.

Traveling with such a person is like driving with someone constantly looking over your shoulder and usually, that's exactly what the Hopelessly Impatient one is doing.

At any rate, this type of difficult person needs to be shown that exhibiting impatience doesn't get you to your destination any faster.

As for dealing with such behavior in public, the first step is to remove the Hopelessly Impatient one from the negative situation. This can best be done by whispering in your traveling companion's ear something like, "Could we step around the corner for a minute? We need to talk."

Next, in a reassuring manner, remind the Hopelessly Impatient one that this is a vacation, not a shooting match. Offer solutions like, "I'll talk to the desk clerk about this myself. You know, these guys get so busy, it's easy to see how a misunderstanding could occur. Let me find out if the hotel can make other arrangements for us."

Maintaining a cool balance is paramount in situations like these. Personally, I avoid them by not using the toll-free reservation numbers. Instead, I call the hotel directly. For some reason, that avoids the whole tedious problem altogether.

If the Hopelessly Impatient one fails to comply with your requests, a reminder that rarely is anything accomplished by public displays of upset and frustration may be needed. Point out that the only thing to come of behavior like that is fatigue—for everyone involved.

The Road to Hell

My friend Marcy and I recently flew to Boston, then rented a car and drove to Maine. From the moment the plane took off to the moment I dropped her off on her doorstep, she complained. Nothing, it seemed, was good enough for her. The plane ride was "sooo uncomfortable,"; the food, "not all it was cracked up to be"; and the rental car, "too small." I wanted to choke her—it was like a vacation from Hell. Things were so miserable for me that I locked myself in the hotel bathroom for a half hour of peace each day.
—Diane S.

Locking yourself in a room to get away from the Whiner-Complainer is a common method of escape—in fact, it's probably why door locks were invented in the first place!

Your first step in dealing with Whiners on Wheels is to remain calm. It's quite tempting to let the anger build up within you, even to become a Volcano. But getting angry with the Whiner will only make things worse because such humiliation only makes them wallow and sulk all the more.

47

Take deep breaths, exhaling them slowly. After a few minutes of practicing your breathing technique, ask the Whiner to explain which problems are the drawbacks to the vacation. Listen attentively, then in a calm manner ask what the Whiner has liked so far. Be careful not to sound sarcastic with this one—it's easy to do.

Certainly, the Whiner will find at least one thing that's been pleasant about the trip, but that's not important. Your asking is the key to making the Whiner readjust his or her thinking, if only for a minute—which is long enough for you to make your point.

Next, say that although the Whiner's opinions are important to you, you would appreciate it if he or she would keep a list of them—to be discussed after you're home. Let the Whiner know that this vacation is important to you and that you'd really appreciate it if stress could be kept to a minimum. After all, isn't that why you both took the time off in the first place?

The Know-it-all

Every year we go on an R.V. trip with five other couples. Last year, we met a new couple, Bob and Cheryl. Cheryl is a quiet, warm person—but Bob is really hard to be around because he thinks he knows everything. When we have map conferences and try to decide on campgrounds, he always mentions his six years of R.V. travel and says he knows where all the good places are. The rest of us are kind of adventuresome; we prefer to explore new places each time we're out. Bob will be traveling with our group again this year, but we're uneasy about going until we find out how to deal with him.

—Lee M.

Know-it-alls always flash their credentials when they are trying to establish their authority on certain subjects. It's a wonder many of them don't rent billboards.

Traveling with a Know-it-all in tow is something akin to driving on autopilot because you lack the freedom to explore or make choices about places to go and things to see.

Your first step in dealing with this difficult type is to set a positive tone while stressing the fact that you're traveling as a team. The opinions of the Know-it-all and the rest of the team are equally equally important, so be careful not to completely ignore the Know-it-all. Being ignored only makes a Know-it-all talk louder.

Next, ask each team member where you should go next. If necessary, take a vote. If the Know-it-all questions any of your actions, calmly say that you're merely taking into account the feelings of all involved because it's not fair for one person to decide what the team is going to do.

Remember: Do not exclude the Know-it-all from any part of the trip's planning sessions. The real object is to achieve fairness, not to punish one troublesome team member.

The Explosive Trip

My husband gets so uptight when we travel that I don't want to go on vacations anymore. He gets so angry over little things, and when he drives his knuckles are so white and his neck is so tense that he can't sleep later. On the last trip, I asked if we could stop for a soda, and he yelled, "Didn't you drink anything before we left?" I feel myself tensing up around him only on vacations—he's not like this as much at home.

—Jeanne M.

Volcanos exhibit signs of stress more quickly and more dramatically than anyone else. These signs are both verbal and physical, and a Volcano can be downright scary to have beside you in the driver's seat of a moving vehicle.

It is easy to respond to the Volcano with a comment like, "If you're going to be like this, then I won't travel with you anymore," but that only tends to make the molten lava bubble.

Instead, the Volcano must be addressed in a quiet, neutral place—such as the hotel room or at home before leaving. Calmly ask the Volcano to sit next to you on the couch or a chair next to yours. Then, in a soothing voice, express your worries over the Volcano's unhealthy outbursts. Here's an example of the discussion you might have:

- YOU: Brian, you really worry me when we're traveling together because you get so angry over little things that don't matter. What is it that's stressing you out about vacations?

- BRIAN: (defensively) I don't get that mad . . .

- YOU: My perception is that you do. It makes me tense, too. Come on, let's talk about it so we can figure out how to make things better for both of us.

- BRIAN: Well, maybe I am tense when we're going somewhere because I hate that in-between part—I just want to get where we're going.

Now you've got a good start on solving the problem. The Volcano has been made aware of his actions, has taken a quick look within, and has offered an explanation for his behavior.

All that's left to do is to determine what you want to

achieve, set some goals, and then get on with the business of enjoying your vacation together. To accomplish this, you can make a simple, straightforward plan like, "You work on controlling your temper, and I'll work on being more understanding and soothing." Or, you can make it a game: "Every time you blow up like that, you will be sentenced to five minutes of having to say only nice things."

Finding what works within the context of your relationship is up to *both* of you.

For Happier Trails . . .

Above all else, try to maintain a sense of humor. You'll need it to get through the less desirable aspects of your vacation. Remember, wherever there are people, there are problems. It's how you deal with these problems that determines how quickly they'll go away.

Remember what your mother told you:
If you can't say anything nice
about someone, then just
say nothing at all.

Part III

Dealing with
Difficult Strangers

Five

Let the Buyer Beware

Shopping has become one of the most stressful things we do—especially during holidays or special sales events.

Yet, it seems as if back in the days of the earliest known shoppers, the hunters and gatherers, conflicts weren't nearly as abundant as they are now.

Today's shopper ventures through the thick, deep corridors of the mall not only out of necessity, but also for a primary social/recreational activity.

From a sociological standpoint, we've become a "fast food" society. We expect everything *now* and our inexhaustible need for instant gratification makes us far more impatient than our predecessors, and far more likely to run into difficult situations, especially with half of the eight types of difficult people.

The best advice I can give you is to leave the most difficult types at home. This will work much of the time—although, obviously, there will be some occasions when you simply cannot avoid shopping with a Hopelessly Impatient or a Catatonic Unresponsive person.

But what about the strangers who work at the mall? Isn't the customer always king? While that is a nice management philosophy, the truth is that mall employees are human beings, too. And human beings get stressed out. What follows are some examples from "shopping Hell."

Are We Done Yet?
Shopping with the Hopelessly
Impatient

My husband says he likes to go to the mall with me, but after we're there a short while he starts to get a little uptight. I like to start at one end of the mall, then look into each store along the way. About ten stores in, he'll start sighing heavily; after fifteen, he starts asking if we're done yet. It makes me nervous to shop with him, and lately I've found that I'm much better off going by myself. And yet, he still says he likes to go with me. I'm not sure how we can work this out.

—Christine L.

The Hopelessly Impatient don't like to window shop—they generally have a one-track mind (e.g., "We're here to buy a pair of jeans, not window shop!"). Many men fall into this category, although it is not uncommon for women to be Hopelessly Impatient as well.

Here's an easy game plan for dealing with the Hopelessly Impatient shopper:

- State the problem in a brief, non-accusatory manner. For example: "We have different ways of shopping. I prefer to take my time, and you seem to want to move things along faster."
- Next, offer a simple solution. One that is pretty effective is, "How about I go my way, you go yours, and we meet in the center concourse in one hour?"
- Finally, stress that you are not angry with the Hopelessly Impatient person, you are only presenting these ideas in an effort to please both of you.

A-Whining We Will Go

It's so hard to get help in stores today! I just went to a hardware store to buy paint, and when I asked the clerk for help, he whined and said, "Ohhh . . . don't you know what you want?" He then walked slowly to the paint section, sighing heavily the whole way. It was like I was interrupting his nap time! It was really unnerving.

—Mary Lou L.

Whiners are not happy people to be around while shopping, mostly because the sheer tone of their voice can easily reduce you to the same level. The only difference is, you'll be whining about the Whiner.

When you encounter a store clerk who is a Whiner, the best thing you can do is politely ask if you were interrupting anything. If clerk says no but still whines, then you must get assertive and ask what the problem is.

Here's how a typical conversation might go:

- YOU: (gently, yet firmly) I really need help with this. But it seems like you're not too interested in answering my questions. It's your job to help me, isn't it?
- CLERK: (taken aback) I . . . I don't know what you mean. I'm helping you, aren't I?
- YOU: You are, but you're kind of whining about it. Don't you have the time to help?
- CLERK: Yes, ma'am.

Be direct but polite when talking about the problem. The worst thing you can do is sound accusatory and angry. Anger only breeds more anger—it never accomplishes anything, and it wastes a lot of time.

Mt. Vesuvius of the Mall

The other day I was in the credit office of a department store, and the guy at the window next to me exploded in anger when the clerk told him he couldn't use his credit card because he was more than thirty days late with his payment. He started screaming at her, said he wasn't going to shop at the #@!* store and then tore up his credit card right in front of everybody. It was really quite embarrassing to watch, and the clerk responded in an alarming way. She screamed back, "Sir, if you'd pay your bill on time, you wouldn't run into problems like this!" This made him angrier, and he called for the manager, who reprimanded the employee.

—Mary T.

Volcanos have a low tolerance level in most things, losing their patience so quickly that you wonder if they ever really had any.

With Volcanos you don't know, it is almost impossible to intervene, so I would advise against getting involved in difficult situations that arise between Volcanos and other people. Let a store manager or someone else in authority break it up. For some reason, Volcanos do respond to authority figures.

If you do decide to become involved (or have no choice in the matter), the *last* thing you want to do is yell back—all that does is add more gasoline to the fire, as well as reward the Volcano's behavior with more of the same. Remember, they *enjoy* shouting matches.

Don't threaten Volcanos or talk down to them with words like, "You sit down over there until I can get the manager," because this only makes them angrier. The primary way Volcanos react to this kind of humiliation (or express any other painful emotion, for that matter) is by exploding at whomever they believe is the perpetrator.

So, before dealing with a Volcano, take a minute and use some mental imagery: Picture a fire; the only way to put it out is by throwing water on it. Imagine the calming, refreshing waves of the water as you toss it on to the fire, putting it out completely.

Now, picture yourself being the water to your Volcano's fire: Using a soothing voice, you will calm and comfort that person. You can achieve this much more easily by practicing this exercise when you are alone and then trying it out on a Volcano—the next time you run into one.

After dealing with the Volcano, do something to relieve the stress that has spilled over onto you as a result of your close encounter with the fire: Drive through the park; have a relaxing lunch at your favorite restaurant. Reward yourself for not blowing up.

A Bully-ish Market

I've shopped in one particular store for a long time, and the lady in the dress department has always been very helpful. Lately, though, she's been pushing some dresses on me that I really don't like, telling me that I "had to buy them" because they were "definitely me." It's getting on my nerves, and I'm starting to think about shopping elsewhere.
—Elaine R.

Bullys like to be in charge of every event they take part in. Worse yet, they delight in making you think that their ideas are *yours*.

Dealing with a "mall Bully" is not as bad as you might think, though. Your first step is to acknowledge the problem, out loud and in front of the Bully. Do this in a quiet setting, such as the entrance to a dressing room, as long as you are away from other customers.

Tell the Bully salesclerk that you've noticed her behavior, and that you would like to know if there is a reason for it. Maybe the store has put the clerk on commission sales only, or maybe new sales quotas have been set for the employees in each department. These are very common reasons for such overt Bully tactics.

Bullys do need to feel like their ideas are important, so don't forget that during your talk. And never talk down to Bullys either—their egos can't stand it. Instead, briefly state the problem, then follow it up with suggestions for the kind of service you would like to receive. After all, if you're a good customer, you deserve to choose how you should be treated.

Remember, rarely does anyone win an argument with a Bully—that's why it's important to avoid arguing with a Bully in the first place. Instead, focus on relating, finding common ground, and working toward a fair solution.

Home Is Where the Catatonic Unresponsive Belongs

Every once in a while, my husband will go shopping with me, but his heart really isn't in it. He drags his feet and rarely shows any emotion at all. He barely talks the whole time, and I feel like I'm dragging around a dead weight. What should I do?

—Alice M.

The only place for a Catatonic Unresponsive to be during shopping expeditions is home. Otherwise, you're both guaranteed to have a bad experience.

There is only one way for you to deal with Catatonic Unresponsive shoppers: Shop for them.

Write down all of your Catatonic's sizes, keep the list on a card in your wallet, and shop alone for this person. One more piece of advice: Whenever possible, use credit cards; they make returns much easier.

**Difficult people are given to us
as a test of our understanding
of the human condition.**

Six

Tangled in
Red Tape—Government
Offices

Only the United States government can bring together
people from all walks of life, leave them in a room for
hours without helping them, and get away with it.

Understaffing in government offices like post offices and
employment bureaus is typical. It seems that, despite all the
taxes we pay, there's never enough money to hire that one
extra employee these offices always seem to need.

Tensions can easily rise at government agencies for a
wide variety of reasons, but the major one is that customers
must often sit for hours, which leads to some difficult

situations with some *very* irritable people. Such tense people often affect the government employees, too.

The Hopelessly Impatient

I was standing in line at the Bureau of Employment Services when the man behind me suddenly started sighing loudly and shifting his weight back and forth. He kept saying, "Oh, come on!" over and over again. This went on for about ten minutes, until I couldn't stand it anymore and I turned to him and said, "Look, would you please stop it? This line isn't going to move any faster, so we might as well make the best of it."

—*Tom D.*

The Hopelessly Impatient is the most common of the eight difficult types to be found in government offices, largely because of the long waiting periods—which can make just about anybody crazy.

The best way to handle the Hopelessly Impatient is to suggest that impatience does not usually bring rewards. Always stress that instead, impatient behavior only breeds more impatience—and makes a bad situation worse. Showing that *you* are patient with the Hopelessly Impatient can be an inspiring way to help get the idea across.

If necessary, you can try to point out the humor in the situation (I always smile and say things like, "I guess these are our tax dollars at work") or make an attempt to strike up a conversation that focuses on something different (e.g., "What part of town are you from?").

If all else fails, tell Hopelessly Impatients to keep their complaints to themselves—at least until you've completed your business.

A Bully Amongst Us

Yesterday I went to the social security office to change my name because of my recent marriage. There were lots of people there; all took numbers and remained seated until their number was called. Everything was okay until a man and his son walked in. The man, who didn't take a number, just stepped up to the clerk's desk and demanded to be helped "right this minute" or else he'd ask to see the manager. A few people protested, and the clerk told him he'd have to take a number—and that the manager would tell him that anyway. He continued to threaten her; she got the manager, who told the man to leave if he could not comply with the rules. It was a tense time for all of us.

—Lisa C.

The Bully holds the belief that he (or she) is always entitled to be first in any line, and always thinks there is a perfectly sound reason for this belief (e.g., "I'm in a hurry," "I'm not feeling too well," "I'll only be a minute," etc.).

It is not uncommon for Bullys to promenade into a room, march up to wherever the people of importance are, and begin making pronouncements that indicate their profound delusions of grandeur.

In government-office situations, Bullys tend to skip the "little things," like taking a number and waiting in line for attention, asking someone what the office's procedures are, or reading the signs that have the seemingly endless instructions on them. No, Bullys feel that they are far more important than anyone else—and that they are entitled to preferential treatment just because of whom (or in this case *what*) they are.

If you are employed by the government agency, you must

almost immediately address the problems that Bullys can create because the longer they wait, the more they feel justified in demanding service before everyone else. You should firmly say, "Excuse me—but you'll have to take a number and wait like everyone else."

If that incites angry comments from the Bully (who, as a kid, was always the one who said "*Make* me!"), your next move, after restating your position, is to force the Bully's attention to those already waiting for service. Their glares alone should achieve the desired effect. Bullys never like to be outnumbered because that usually counters what the Bullys ultimately hope to accomplish, which is consensus and conformity to their own personal beliefs.

Take away the Bully's support system (real or hopeful) and you can avoid a negative situation. Try to nip this one in the bud. The sooner you do, the less justification the Bully has for reacting negatively.

P.O.'d at the P.O.

I was at the post office yesterday and the guy in front of me did something I still can't believe. When his turn came, he approached the clerk's desk in what seemed to be okay spirits. Then, when the clerk told him that his box would cost $10 to mail, he blew up. He called her a name I can't repeat, then said he'd drive the package to whomever he was going to send it to. Everyone was looking at him, but he didn't even seem to notice. His face was red because he was mad, not because he was embarrassed!

—Helen M.

Volcanos have notoriously short fuses, and they often explode at things you or I would take in stride.

Often, Volcanos explode and then abruptly leave the room, never to be seen or heard from again, but they have also been known to stick around to try to win their self-proposed battles.

So, how can people deal with Volcanos in public places without becoming new bombing targets themselves? In these cases, it is usually best to let the fuse burn itself out—then try to get the Volcano to calm down. You might gently ask if he or she is all right or offer to help in any way you can.

More often than not, the public Volcano will prefer to be left alone—and usually is, anyway.

Remember: *Never* try to defuse a bomb while it's still ticking.

Tuning In to the Non-Listener

I was at the Bureau of Motor Vehicles last week because I needed a new driver's license. The government clerk kept asking me the same question over and over again. Since she was a little too young to be senile, I soon realized that she simply didn't know how to listen. Yet, I still became quite upset with her, particularly when she began talking over me while I was trying to explain the situation to her. Finally, I got the manager to help me because I'd just never dealt with anyone like that before.

—Sondra J.

There's no doubt about it—Non-Listeners are among the most frustrating difficult people to deal with. That's because you have to contend with two separate (but related) problems: (1) Non-Listeners lack listening skills altogether.

(2) Non-Listeners never stop talking long enough for anyone to really answer their questions.

Your first step is to get the Non-Listener's attention. You may do this by silently staring at the perpetrator until he or she is forced to *ask* for a response to the question; or you may interject loudly (but *not* in a hostile manner) with a two-word cue, such as, "Please listen." It is important that you remember to be polite, yet firm.

(As in all other difficult encounters, *do* try to maintain your equilibrium. In other words, try not to lose your temper, no matter how easy or understandable that may be.)

Once you've got the Non-Listener's attention, hold on to it by stating calmly that he or she may not speak until you are through. In as nice a tone as possible, say something like, "Please wait until I'm through giving you the information you need—and don't interrupt me."

Next, state your thoughts or provide your information as succinctly as possible. (Remember: Although you have the Non-Listener's somewhat-undivided attention, moments like these do not last long, so speak clearly, positively, and accurately.)

One more thing you should try to keep in mind is that Non-Listeners were probably never taught how to listen to or converse with other people. These are skills that many of us take for granted, but Non-Listeners were deprived of learning them—probably by other Non-Listeners. Many times, it's a family trait.

Also, there is the unfortunate fact that people who lack communications skills are often (and ironically) the very ones in positions of power.

Keep a cool head and try not to lose your patience with the Non-Listener. Instead, try to be sympathetic and understanding.

A Brief Reminder

Above all else, remember that a healthy sense of humor is your strongest ally when you're all tangled up in government red tape (situations that are almost always difficult). Sometimes, there's very little you can do to remove yourself from tough moments—so it's up to you to make the best of things. If you can laugh about it, you'll find that the time passes more quickly, and you'll feel much better after your business is completed.

Difficult people will test you
to your limit—it's your
responsibility to set realistic
boundaries to keep discussions in
check.

Seven

Home, Sweet . . . Home?
Difficult Landlords

If a man's home is his castle, then a rented home or apartment can often be a dungeon. Why? Because, in the deep, dark realms of the rental industry, three of the eight difficult types often rear their ugly heads.

On a more serious note, landlord-tenant conflicts can be quite trying and time-consuming, especially if the renter is inexperienced or has since moved away. But there are several ways to deal with difficult landlords, some practical and others legal.

The Bully-winner:
A Deadly Combination

I recently moved to another city. My old landlord sent me a letter stating that he was only returning $135 of my security deposit, not the full $325 he owed me. I had been a good tenant. I'd paid my rent on time and left the place very clean. But the landlord deducted $190 for cleaning expenses and the repair of a "damaged" refrigerator coil. I had three cats, which he had said was okay, but in the letter he threw that back in my face and said, "I guess three cats throw off a lot of hair."

This kind of Bully-Whiner combination can be very taxing to deal with, because you have to take into account all of the aspects of each type, combine them, and then try to figure out a workable strategy.

I had had previous clues to my ex-landlord's behavior, so I was not that shocked by such a letter. I knew he was a Bully because twice, in the brief time I rented from him, he had entered my apartment—without notice or any emergency reason—when I wasn't home. How did I know? I had put a small piece of clear tape across the bottom of the door (a là the T.V. Show *The Rockford Files*) and when I came home on those occasions, I saw that the tape had been broken. So, I documented that. (I also let him know about it when he refused to return all of my security deposit.)

Also, whenever the landlord came around when I was home, his arrival was usually unannounced, and he was usually whining about something—whether it was about fixing the cracks on my walls or why he'd bought the place at all. These were my first clues to his being a Whiner.

Here's how I handled the security-deposit situation: First, I sent him a registered letter, stating that I had not cashed his check because I was waiting for the full amount. Then I sent a photocopy of the lease agreement, which had only one rule of departure—thirty days written notice, which I had given. I also noted that the lease said nothing about cleaning, which I had done anyway, as a courtesy.

Next, I tackled the refrigerator problem. I called the appliance maker's consumer hotline and asked an engineer if the refrigerator coils could have been bent by failing to defrost the unit, as the Bully-Whiner had suggested. The engineer said the only way to bend the coils was by chipping away at the ice with a knife—something I could not have done since I had forgotten to defrost the unit. The engineer offered an affidavit to that effect, and I told my ex-landlord about it in my letter.

There is a "fair wear and tear" clause in many states' landlord/tenant laws. Basically, this means that general upkeep of the rental unit is the responsibility of the landlord or owner, and not something you can be penalized for later unless you did indeed cause provable damage to the property.

Be sure to look up such state laws when you're dealing with difficult landlords. There will be case histories on file that set the state's precedents for dealing with particular rental situations, and if you can cite a case number in your letter you'll find that your landlord will likely respond in your favor, because the law is the law.

Finally, I ended my letter on a more positive note— because the object is to achieve fairness, not to out-Bully the Bully. (That's an important distinction to keep in mind.) I told my landlord that he seemed to be a reasonable person and that I hoped the matter could be settled without further incident.

He called me and said, in a nice way, that I was had been a good tenant, after all. Then he sent me the check.

My meticulous documentation helped a great deal, but I really believe it was the nice tone I offered at the end of my letter that brought about a pleasant end to this otherwise nasty situation. It pays to be a little patient, understanding, and human.

If I had attacked him like a Volcano or a Bully, we would have locked horns further and perhaps not reached a settlement as quickly—or perhaps not without the help of the court system.

Giving Bullys or Whiners a taste of their own medicine never works—it just validates their feelings that their own behavior is justified. Appealing to their sense of decency and having an air of forgiveness in your own words, makes all the difference in the world. This creates an atmosphere that encourages correct behavior because you are neither demanding an apology nor threatening an attack.

More About the Winning Landlord

My landlord has begun calling me one or two days in advance of when the rent is due and asking in a very whiny tone if I'll be paying the rent on time this month. The fact is, I've never once been late with a payment! I consider this borderline harassment, and it really makes me angry—so angry that I've started looking for another place to live."
—Dean R.

Let's face it, Whiner-Complainers are downright nasty to be around. Just the sound of their voice can put knots in your stomach.

What Whiners are most worried about is . . . well, worrying. That's their primary concern in life. When they're not worried about one thing in particular, they're worried about the fact that they're not worried.

So, how do you deal with Whiner-Complainer landlords? You start by asking a few questions, like:

- Have I ever forgotten to pay the rent on time?
- Why do you find it necessary to call me every month? It says in our lease agreement that the rent isn't due till the first of each month, and I've already shown that I can comply with that.
- Did a previous tenant cause you problems? Is that why you call me—to protect yourself against a repeat offender? If so, can you please try to separate that past experience from me?

Always stress that, aside from these calls that trouble you, you've have a decent landlord-tenant relationship, one that needn't be affected by the Whiner's behavior—once it ceases.

Remember: Whiners are the easiest ones to kill with kindness.

The Catatonic
Unresponsive Landlord

My toilet keeps running and I've called the landlord about it repeatedly. He always says he'll be out to look at it, but he never comes. Nothing's been done for eight weeks. Once before, I wound up having to call a plumber and deduct the bill from my rent. My landlord reprimanded me for doing this, but I don't think I have any other options.

—Juanita L.

Catatonic Unresponsive landlords are the easiest type to deal with, even though they are the most difficult ones to approach at first.

You must understand that Catatonic Unresponsives live in constant fear of making the wrong decisions. That's why they prefer that you make the decisions for them, even if they complain about it later.

Deducting repair bills from the rent is one way to deal with such a landlord—but make sure to keep all the bills and send a copy of each one along with the rest of your monthly rent.

If the Catatonic Unresponsive reprimands you for doing this, ask why the problem wasn't addressed when you first mentioned it.

The next time a situation like this arises you might first want to set an appointment for the landlord to look at the problem. At the time you set it up let the landlord know that you will take action if the appointment isn't kept. Again, this could come in the form of deducting the amount of the bill, or you could place your rent money in escrow until the problem is properly addressed.

Again, check your state's landlord/tenant laws for additional information.

A Brief Note About
Bad Neighbors

As a tenant, you have the right to live in a quiet building, free of harassment from any of your neighbors. If you have any Bully or Volcano neighbors who are bothering you, check your lease. It should state that you have the option of reporting such disturbances to your landlord, who should take appropriate action.

It's not what you are, it's *how* you are what you are that counts.

Part IV

Notes
on Long-term
Survival

Eight

If the Shoe Fits . . .
How to Avoid Being a
Difficult Person

═══════════════════════════════════════

Have your co-workers left you out of their once-a-week lunches? Has your husband been spending more time "watching the game with the boys"? Have you noticed that people start inching away from you whenever you air what you consider to be a legitimate gripe?

These are subtle signs that you may have joined the ranks of difficult people. If you have, this chapter will clue you in to those behaviors and character traits that you may not yet be aware of—and, hopefully, will lead you to think before you speak and act in the future.

The Six Red Flags:
Or, How to Tell When You're
Being Difficult

These are the six warning signs that you may be a difficult person:

1. People around you start making themselves scarce.
2. Your family tells you outright that you're being difficult.
3. The people you're complaining to just nod and ignore you, as if they've heard what you're saying before.
4. People start agreeing with you just so you'll shut up.
5. Invitations to work or family functions are suddenly few and far between.
6. Even the dog won't listen to you anymore.

Okay, so you've been experiencing three of the six above-mentioned warning signs. You still don't believe it. What can you do next to prove to yourself that you are, indeed, a difficult person?

Ask the people around you. They've been observing your behavior for much longer than you've been aware of it. They have witnessed you at your worst. They have even, in some cases, voiced the opinion that you're in danger of losing your friends, or even your job.

You weren't ready to listen to them before. But, all of a sudden, it seems that some of the things they've warned you about have happened. You've lost your best friend, or you got fired because of your temper or your impatience or your inability to listen. Now you want to know what's wrong so you can fix it. You want to move boldly into a future where you no longer repeat the patterns that have led to the horrible mess you're in now.

Asking for Feedback

Start by asking your family, because they have the best information about your regular behavior patterns. After all, they probably see more of you than others do. Remain calm when you ask them which "difficult" characteristics you've been displaying the most. Also, have them describe the ones that seemed hurtful to them. Next, write all these down in a notebook.

Then you should interview your friends and co-workers. Make it very clear that you don't want to hear polite little remarks like, "Oh, there's nothing wrong with you." You need cold, hard facts in order to determine what about your behavior needs radical change and what simply needs a little work.

Most important, this kind of personal investigation requires you to learn how to take criticism—and it also requires your friends to learn how to give it.

To take criticism well, you need to remember that these comments are being offered to help you. They are only small pieces of the information that you need to piece together the larger puzzle of why your behavior is being perceived as difficult.

Your friends will need a few ground rules for offering their criticism. They should confine their comments to specifics and not add every single gory detail they can think of. They need to know that this is not their golden opportunity to blast you for every thing you've ever done wrong, rather, it is your time to find out what's wrong and how to fix it.

After you've completed your fact-finding mission, sit in a private place and read through your notes. Do you see a pattern? Are the certain characteristics that all or most of your subjects mentioned repeatedly? Discovering your behavior patterns is the first step toward breaking them.

Exchanging Negative Ideas
for Positive Ones

You can start exchanging negative ideas for positive ones by keeping a journal. It will help you become aware of particular situations that make you a Volcano, Bully, Whiner or other type. It needn't be too elaborate; a chart like the one in the following example is effective.

In Column 1 include the day, date, and time the event occurred. This will help you to find out if particular days or times of the day present problems for you. For instance, you might notice that you tend to become a Volcano on Monday mornings more often then at any other time. Again, establishing that you have such patterns is the first step toward breaking them.

Label Column 2 "Event" (or "Stimulus"), and write a brief description of the situation that you feel prompted your behavior. A typical entry might read: "Woman stepped in front of me in line at the post office" or "Joe S. got the promotion I thought I deserved." Keep it as simple as possible, because reducing the situation to its lowest common denominator will help you in determining whether it was worth the trouble and upset.

The third column, under the heading "Current Response/Behavior," should detail your *present* reaction to the situations described in the second column. Do not cheat here by including what you *should* have done; save that for Column 5. Again short descriptions work best, as in the following: "Face got red. Palms got sweaty. Felt about to burst, then shouted 'Stop it, you idiot!' at man next to me on bus."

Column 4, entitled "How Others Responded," is about the innocent victims. Here, include observations like, "Man's face turned red, then he got up and left" or "Sheila said I was out of line, then hung up on me." This will help you to become sensitive to the feelings of others involved in the situation.

Finally, the fifth column is for "Positive Options/ Alternatives"—the behavior you wish you had exhibited at the time (if you had it to do over again) or how you hope to react the next time the event occurs. Column 5 is the place for longer and more detailed answers: "I will sit calmly, take long, deep breaths, and then I will really listen to the other person's words carefully before shooting my mouth off"; or "Next time, I will go to my office alone for a few minutes, count to ten, and calm down before resuming the meeting.

Date/Time	Event	Current Response/ Behavior
11/16. 9 A.M.	Son spilled milk	Yelled at him
12/3. 11 A.M.	Clerk helped another client first	Seethed, then gave a piece of my mind when my turn came
1/17. 4 P.M.	Huge phone bill came	Screamed at daughter

How Others Responded	Positive Options/Alternatives
He cried	I will be more understanding in the future—after all, this happens to everyone
She apologized but was visibly shaken	It was an honest mistake. I will take a deep breath, then try to forget about it
She yelled back, then ran out of the house	We will calmly discuss why we can't afford high phone bills

Remember, above all to try to have a sense of humor about each situation—after all, you're only human.

Form A New Habit

If you get into the habit of keeping this kind of journal on a daily or weekly basis, you'll start to see that, like everyone else, you're pretty much a creature of habit. We all have intricate webs of patterned behaviors and responses The object of keeping the journal is to develop awareness of the *negative* patterns in our lives so that we can recognize and free ourselves (and others) from these.

The "Today I will . . ." Jar

Keeping a "Today I Will . . ." jar is another helpful exercise. On a blank piece of paper, write down twenty-five positive thoughts. Then cut these up into separate strips of paper, fold them, and put them into a jar.

Always start each one with the words "Today I

will . . ." For example: "Today I will listen to all ideas presented to me before I offer mine" or "Today I will take my time and be more patient about everything."

Every day, pull out one strip of paper, read its message, and try to live up to it throughout that particular day. You'll be surprised by how fun a game it can become. Some people I know who use this technique also involve their family members in it as a safeguard against cheating.

Making this kind of positive behavior therapy into a game can make it easier on your ego, too—and you'll eventually get to the point where you won't need little pieces of paper to remind you to be a better person.

Parting Thoughts

- Always remember that the feelings of others are as important as your own.
- Remember what your mother told you: If you can't say anything nice, don't say anything at all.
- Keep your eyes and ears open to your own behavior. Look for the patterns in your responses to certain types of situations. Then do the healthy thing by breaking all the negative patterns.
- Take the observations of those close to you as seriously as if these had come from your own inner voice. Write down every positive alternative to your current behavior and consider many solutions to the problem before settling on one.
- Remember that we all have good days and bad days. Trying to tip the scale toward the good is part of the work of being human.
- All of the tips in this chapter are applicable to every

type of difficult person. As author Richard Bach once said, "You teach best what you most need to learn."

- Learning to laugh at yourself (and others) will help you through difficult circumstances more than you might think. A good laugh takes the sting out of a bad situation.

ABOUT THE AUTHOR

KATINA Z. JONES is co-author of *How to Collect Child Support* (Longmeadow Press) and Markets Editor of *Writer's Digest* magazine. She has written for *McCall's*, *Crain's Cleveland Business*, the (Akron) *Beacon Journal*, the *Cincinnati Post*, and several business and trade journals. Prior to becoming a full-time freelance writer, she was an award-winning editor of *EveryBody's News*, Cincinnati's arts/entertainment bi-weekly. She received her Bachelor of Arts from Kent State University in 1986.

A member of the Author's Guild, Ms. Jones is currently working on a book about ovarian cancer.

She lives in Fairlawn, Ohio, with her husband, Louis Romestant.